MARY ENGELBREIT'S

HOME
COMPANION

collections

MARY ENGELBREIT'S
HOME
COMPANION

collections

Text by Vitta Poplar

Photography by Barbara Elliott Martin

**Andrews McMeel
Publishing**

Kansas City

www.andrewsmcmeel.com
www.maryengelbreit.com

Library of Congress Cataloging-in-Publication Data
Poplar, Vitta.
Collections / text by Vitta Poplar ; photography by Barbara Elliott Martin
    p.cm.
ISBN 0-7407-0684-5
  1. Collectibles in interior decoration. I. Martin, Barbara Elliott. II. Mary Engelbreit's
home companion. III. Title.

NK2115.5.C58P67 2000
745--dc21

                                                                99-462035

First Edition
10 9 8 7 6 5 4 3 2 1

MARY ENGELBREIT'S HOME COMPANION
Editor in Chief: Mary Engelbreit
Executive Editor: Barbara Elliott Martin
Art Director: Marcella Spanogle

Produced by SMALLWOOD & STEWART, INC., New York City

Printed in Spain
D.L. TO: 185-2000

contents

introduction

OVER THE YEARS, I'VE BUILT UP MY SHARE OF COLLECTIONS, foraging with my clan of fellow flea-marketers. In fact, in many cases I didn't even know I was amassing anything until I noticed that I had three of something—which I believe is the official definition of a collection.

Just to keep things interesting, I've moved three times in a period of five years. The first two times, I divested myself of worldly goods in an effort to make a fresh start. . . only to start collecting all over again, often in a completely different area. In one house it would be marble busts; in another, McCoy and dollhouses. By the third move, I gave up and just brought it all along. Santa figures, purses, postcards, Scotties, anything with hearts, vintage cookbooks—the list goes on and on. And so did the moving boxes. And the mover's comments.

I've always believed that if you see something you REALLY like, you should buy it. I've also found that bringing a friend along sweetens the experience—and doubles your chances of picking "that perfect thing that I've always needed though didn't realize it until now" out of a flea market jumble. Happy collecting!

Mary Engelbreit

why collect?

First produced in late Victorian England, chintzware is still made to this day. Most valued of all, however, are the early wares of Royal Winton, like this 1920s casserole (above).

These early 20th century papier-mâché bunny rabbits and eggs are actually hollow containers which were made to hold candy (opposite).

WE'RE ALL DRAWN TO GATHER THINGS FOR personal reasons, some so complex that we don't even understand them ourselves. How to explain a deep-rooted love of salt and pepper shakers or old garden watering cans or tiny dollhouse chairs? No matter what drives us, few are immune to the urge to collect, a passion that can surface as soon as we can walk.

There are not many rules to collecting, beyond selecting what you like and buying the best you can afford. Always look for the earliest version of a particular collectible—for instance, a popular toy that had subtle changes over a thirty-year period—which increases its value. To learn the fine points, read collectibles guides and join collector's clubs. Those freebie antiquing papers also have timely articles on who's buying what now.

If you're mystified by pricing, remember that it is not an exact science. Regional preferences prevail, and trends are an important influence: Witness the rise of Arts and Crafts furniture to astronomic prices. If you have a limited budget, or are looking for bargains, the trick is to stay ahead of the competition.

There are some standard criteria, however, for deter-
mining value. Rarity, condition, age, quality of materials
and workmanship, and history (maybe it once belonged to
someone famous) each play a role. Rarity results from
several factors. Maybe few people saved something (match-
book covers or giveaways, for instance), or it was made by
an artist in small numbers. Outmoded items produced for a
limited period of time have inherent value. One example is
transistor radios from the 1950s with civil defense markings
on the dial. Popularity is also a factor; collectibles go in
and out of vogue and their prices change accordingly. For
instance, American quilts skyrocketed in the 1980s: Chinese-
made copies have since flooded the market, making buyers
wary of authenticity and driving prices down. Collectibles
with crossover appeal tend to be priced high—like teddy
bear cookie jars, which interest jar collectors and bear
lovers alike.

SHOPPING AROUND

Antiques shops offer the best selection, and you'll gain
from someone else's collecting forays, but you'll pay top
dollar for the privilege. Some dealers will consider a
counteroffer below the asking price.

To really put your eye to the test, try flea markets. At
first, the choices seem overwhelming, so you must have a
plan. Get there early. Bring along a wish list, complete
with dimensions, details, and color schemes of what you are
looking for. If you can, survey the entire flea market first,

Displaying collections is
half the fun. Use your
favorite doll, an old
dressmaker's form, or
wooden mannequin as
simultaneous storage
and display for pins and
necklaces (above).

Papier-mâché and
composition cardboard
snowmen from the early
20th century need delicate
handling (opposite).
Fortunately, they're on
display only once a year,
stored the remainder
of the time in acid-free
tissue paper to keep their
own paper content from
deteriorating.

Hand mirrors were once favored souvenir items. This selection—from late 19th-century sterling to 1930s celluloid—reflects a well-traveled owner (above).

Weekend motoring brought wicker baskets like the one in the background, with separate compartments for food storage and a place to stash dishware under the lid, into vogue (opposite). By the 1950s, woven-look tin baskets prevailed.

cruising the aisles with notebook and Polaroid camera to compare and contrast, and jog your memory (this will also help in future junkets).

Dealers usually keep the expensive stuff up front and center. Look under the table and search through boxes. Ask for the "best price." Cash speaks volumes.

AUCTIONS GREAT AND SMALL

"Auction Today: Entire Contents of Home, Including Carriage House" reads the enticing notice. So there you sit, as the auctioneer zips along at eighty lots per hour. "The more you pay, the better it is!" he barks. "Don't lose it."

Well, most of us do. It's easy to get confused. Did those five pewter English mugs really just go for $5? That album of 100 European postcards for $15? Were they worth it? Except for the top houses, most auctions won't guarantee authenticity or even tell you much about a piece. Their catalogs are often mystifying: you'll see prolific use of the word "early" to signify anything pre-1960s. Or you may encounter enigmatic descriptions like "in the style of" or "one good glass lot."

That's why you should always go to the previews and examine everything up close, preferably with a collectibles guidebook in hand. Take notes and establish your bidding limit, keeping in mind that you'll pay an additional buyer's premium, determined by the auction house. Be sure to register early and reserve your seat (bring a folding chair just in case). Auctions can last for hours. In fact, many

people—even dealers—grow tired and leave, and it's not unheard of to pick up something really great for next to nothing at 10:30 on a blustery winter's night.

Of course, now there's a far simpler—if much less colorful—way to build your collection. Bid online and you'll never have to get out of your pajamas. Just like a "real" auction, you register; the sites give the specifics and walk you through the procedures, including details like who pays for postage.

Online auctions can last from a week to a month. Read the descriptions carefully and view the photos, but with healthy skepticism. What means "mint" to someone else could mean "good" to you. Get to know sellers of the kinds of things you collect, and check a seller's reputation through feedback listings before bidding. Learn the abbreviations and terminology of sellers: MIB, for instance, means "mint in box," or about as pristine as an object can be.

View the site's archives for completed auctions to see what similar things have sold for in the past. Since the highest bidder takes the lot, it makes sense to offer your best bid at the outset rather than waiting for the stakes to rise. Try offering $79.25 instead of $79.00 to get yourself an edge over round-numbered bids.

Think of it as a learning experience when you read online descriptions. It may feel remote and unreal, but when you open that box full of Christmas tree pins from the 1950s, all that patient pointing and clicking in front of the computer will seem worth it!

It's less expensive to collect Bakelite flatware patiently, piece by piece, rather than scooping up a fully assembled set (opposite).

Glass-stoppered apothecary bottles were popular throughout the 1900s. Uneven lips and imperfections in the glass indicate great age. Antique bottles are rare, but there are good reproductions (above).

bakelite
revolution

VISITORS TO DR. LEO BAEKELAND'S YONKERS, New York, laboratory in 1907 probably took a step back in surprise. In the middle of the room sat a large, pulsating, egg-like device, from which tubes and coils protruded, emitting steam and a strange smell, and what we today call plastic. Then, it would have been eerily unfamiliar.

Of course, Dr. Baekeland was no mad scientist. With the help of this device, dubbed The Baekelizer, he was marrying phenol and formaldehyde to create a substance that could coat electrical coils. Along the way, he also made a material that would make the world a more colorful, creative place.

Bakelite was a smash. Stronger than celluloid, it was fireproof and did not break easily, yet could take on myriad shapes and colors. Designers of the 1920s and 1930s loved its surreal, polished appearance, which made the thermoplastic perfect for streamlined product design.

Well into the 1940s, Bakelite ruled the home. Pushed to the back of the drawer or stored in the attic in the 1950s, Bakelite jewelry, radios, telephones, and boxes have re-emerged as bright as the day they were poured—just what you'd expect from a miracle material.

Chameleon-like, the "material of one thousand uses" invaded every corner of the home. It not only perched on tables and shelves shaped as telephones, clocks, radios, and electric fans, but also poured into wardrobe closets and jewel boxes as belt buckles, buttons, and pins (above and opposite).

The Bakelite revolution
spawned even a hobby
or two. Costing about
a dollar, mass-produced
1940s mini-cameras
looked like toys but
actually worked, and
made photography
less formidable to the
amateur (right).

Jazz Age women
decked their wrists with
lightweight Bakelite
bracelets, carved to
represent pineapples,
tropical flowers, and
machine age sprockets.
Butterscotch, cocoa,
and cinnabar were
favorite colors (above).

time in a
bottle

origins, even though it's not always spelled out. The 19th- and early 20th-century examples—the kinds that make collectors swoon—have a pontil mark on the bottom, indicating that they were handblown on a rod. They also tend to have tiny bubbles inside. Molded bottles—produced after 1860—have a telltale seam.

Fruit jars (popularly known as Mason jars for John Landis Mason, who introduced his unique screw-on zinc lids in 1858) are especially easy to date: many have a trademark, a patent date, even a factory monogram embossed in the glass. Early jars were simply lettered; later ones had elaborate monograms, even portraits of animals and war heroes, all encased in the most delectably pale shades of teal, sea green, and romantic amber.

Bottles that still bear their labels—for instance, an old liniment or Tabasco sauce container—are especially valuable. If any bottle is discolored with a rainbow patina, it's been in contact with the soil for a long time. This reduces its worth, but—like crazing on an old plate—many collectors find the effect even more beautiful.

Once containing bitters, a cobalt bottle now offers sugar water to bees, a Provençal custom (above).

Care for some Citrate of Magnesia? Blood Renewer? Elixirs such as these once effervesced in deep blue bottles (opposite).

A bottle doesn't have to be old to catch illustrator Pat Brangle's eye. "I look for unusual color, shape, lettering, and embossed designs," she says. Not coincidentally, these are the same qualities that lend collectible bottles some extra value (top left).

Swathed in chrome, soda water bottles are more elegant to the eye. They were probably once part of a hotel bar (bottom left).

Bottles cushioned in wicker were originally popular accessories in picnickers' hampers (right).

Unearthed in a back-
yard, these milk bottles
could date from as early
as the 1930s, though
pyro-glazed and silk-
screened graphics
continued to be made
well into the 1960s.
Note how some have a
bulge near the lip, called
a "cream top." This
indicates they were
made in the pre–World
War II years, before
the milkman began to
make his rounds with
a wire basket that fit
only streamlined bottles.
Red and orange were
the most prolific lettering
colors, though blue,
green, and yellow were
seen too. The bottles'
catchy slogans, nursery
rhymes, and patriotic
messages entertained
children at breakfast.
The cream of the crop—
limited editions for a
particular client—require
the most milk money.

by the
books

IT'S STILL POSSIBLE TO GET IN ON THE
ground floor of book collecting. Unlike many other areas,
prices aren't inflated and the stock is by no means tapped
out. You don't need a lot of money. What you DO need is a
sharp eye, a little knowledge, and lots of determination.

There's no question that the choices are overwhelming.
So make it easier by focusing on just one area. Not just
cookbooks, but dessert cookbooks. Instead of American
history, choose American women's history—very hot with
collectors, by the way. Other sought-after subjects are
"photoplay editions" of books with movie tie-ins (like a
1925 printing of *Moby-Dick* featuring photos of John
Barrymore) and first editions of pre–World War II American
authors like Hemingway, Steinbeck, and Faulkner.

A surprising number of finds do await at library
sales—especially if you pay a small fee for an early viewing.
The copyright and title pages speak volumes. Don't
mistake the author's year of birth for the book's copyright
date! If you see the words "first edition of first printing,"
and it's signed by the author, you're doubtless holding a
small treasure.

All children's books are
charming, but those that
have won the Caldecott
or Newbery Awards (for
illustrations and literature,
respectively) are especially
desirable (opposite).

Many collectors
focus on first editions or
a single topic, but if you
like an old title for its steel
engravings or pretty spine,
that's reason enough to
bring it home (above).

Old cookbooks are a way of time-traveling through history and seeing how tastes (literally) change. Years ago, food preparation was often regarded as a science, rather than an art, as the vaguely chemical illustrations in *The Kitchen People* show (left). Though classic recipes segue from generation to generation, vintage books often turn up clunkers that might have been the "jalapeño poppers" of their day. For instance, the volume entitled *Some Favorite Southern Recipes of the Duchess of Windsor* (above right) could well advocate pairing tea with grits. It's fun to amass several editions of the same book, such as *The Joy of Cooking*, which was copyrighted in 1931 (below right).

In a California writer's home, custom-built bookshelves surround the picture window. Notice that many of the books have their dust jackets, which can increase a book's value tenfold. Dust jackets are a 1920s invention, created by booksellers to dress up their product (and raise prices). In the foreground sits another good investment: lavishly photographed modern-day design books, which often go out of print quickly and escalate rapidly in value as a result.

timeless
clocks

Certain eras of vintage wristwatches are instantly identifiable and highly collectible. Rectangular, subtly curved shapes were a 1930s hallmark, while 1950s watches were decidedly square (above).

Plastic kitchen clocks, a staple in postwar households, introduced bright bursts of color to the walls of many breakfast nooks (opposite).

A CLOCK COLLECTION OFTEN BEGINS IN the most unassuming way. You pick one off a shelf in a secondhand shop, dust if off, wind it, and, miraculously, it starts ticking. Almost like a pet, it begs to be brought home. Then it's only a matter of time before the collection grows. After all, you can actually use them!

Older clocks on the market generally date from the late 1700s onward. The inner workings of these old clocks have a great many wooden parts. As the 19th century progressed, the works were more likely to be made of brass.

But what's inside doesn't so much matter to most collectors as what's outside: the look of the clock cabinet. At the high end, American wall and shelf clocks, which had their heyday from about 1840 to 1880, come in myriad shapes—banjo, double decker, acorn, and beehive among them. And many feature gorgeous decorative details like reverse-painted or etched-glass panels. They often came with a card stuck to the case interior that named the maker, for instance, Seth Thomas or Chauncey Jerome.

And who can resist a cuckoo? The best come from the Black Forest of Germany and were produced from the

mid-19th century until World War II. They're generally unsigned, so look for the classic gabled roof, a bell or gong accompanying the cuckoo call, and the bird made of painted wood, sometimes with moveable wings and beak.

Many collectors seek pure novelty, like the animated clocks of the first half of the 20th century. Well known examples are cats and clowns whose eyes move back and forth, while a tail or necktie swings as a pendulum. The biggest maker was Lux and early cases were made of pressed wood and metal, later ones of plastic.

If you want to collect on a small scale, look into the world of watches and alarm clocks. You'll probably be surprised to learn, for instance, that alarm clocks have been around since 1690, when they appeared as jewel-encrusted pocket watches carried by the French elite (they didn't necessarily work very well). You can sometimes determine the date by inscriptions or engravings on the outer case that make historical reference. Wristwatches came into vogue in the early 20th century and kept pace with each decade's design trends. Collectors prize designs by well-known makers like Rolex, Baume & Mercier, and Piguet.

Clock collectors often buy from auctions and classified ads. But clocks can be found in thrift shops and, on junk night in your town, keep an eye out for a friendly dial peeking out among the old sinks. Strangely, many people discard old mantel or wall models when all they need is a little TLC. Still, even if the clock never ticks again, it hardly matters, since the face is timeless.

In the first decades of the 20th century, alarm clocks sported twin bells on top (opposite).

Displaying pocket watches is often a conundrum: one collector solved the problem by propping a pocket watch alarm clock on a tiny easel (above). The subsidiary second dial and stainless steel body identify it as 19th century, as earlier watches were either silver or gold, without second dials.

Hinged to open back-to-back, these early 20th-century twin bank clocks (left) were designed to accommodate passersby in both directions on Main Street. Their faces make it easy to see why clocks have been described as "mechanical pictures."

With the invention of celluloid in the late 19th century, most clock cases—and false teeth—no longer had to be made of wood. Witness this sleek Deco-era clock, with its sophisticated subsidiary dial to mark each passing second (above).

37

animal
magnetism

When Fala bounded into the White House in the 1940s, Scotties became a favorite motif of home furnishing designers (above).

Ozark crafter Vicki Rotramel offers sock-monkey history: "They were a big fad in the 1920s and 1930s, when the red-heeled sock was introduced. People patched and made toys from the worn ones (opposite)."

AS RESPONSIBLE COLLECTORS KNOW, EVEN the strictest "no pets" policy can't bar sheep or even elephants from living happily and openly in your home. Menageries in china, fabric, plastic, and wood are always allowed.

Start your own barnyard, complete with red roosters on 1950s cocktail napkins and "Swanky Swigs" drinking glasses, milk glass hens on nests, piggie banks, cow creamers and paintings, duck cookie jars, and horse figurines.

You're going to need some dogs. There's no shortage of china bulldogs and terrier sconces, bloodhound butlers and dachshund needlepoint pillows. . . but the inside canine crowd specializes in genuine, authentic paraphernalia— 18th-century collars, medallions, and badges from dog shows around the world, silver Victorian grooming tools, even pottery food bowls from the 1930s.

Cats, by contrast, are harder to sniff out. Only after turn-of-the-20th-century English artist Louis Wain got the yarnball rolling with his illustrations of cats engaged in human activities did felines become popular. Thereafter, chalkware carnival prizes, teapots, and postcards took up residence in collectors' homes.

From the late 19th century to World War I, glassy-eyed, felt-covered German papier-mâché cow and sheep pulltoys were popular in America (left).

Scottie fever first struck when Louis Icart, the French Deco artist, created several popular prints. The dog soon appeared in magazine ads, comic strips, and books including *Thy Servant a Dog* by Rudyard Kipling and Marjorie Flack's *Angus* series. Decorative figurines (top right), tumbler sets, napkins, and lunch boxes also trotted into the home.

Sewn from antique fabric, artist Stacey Stucky's miniature teddy bears (bottom right) follow in a tradition begun by Morris Michtom, a Brooklynite who introduced the stuffed bear in 1910.

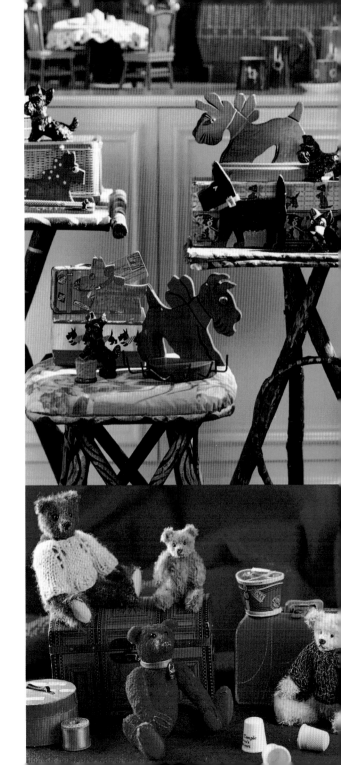

all the right
buttons

WE TEND TO THINK OF BUTTONS AS FUNCTIONAL, but they were once everyone's secret good luck charm.

In Louisa May Alcott's day, girls strung buttons together on silk cords in the belief that if they could somehow assemble 999 different types, the man of their dreams would appear. Older ladies in the crowd lured swains with velvet-backed perfume buttons, which they'd dab with jasmine or violet water. Don't think men were above button bewitchery: they sported sparkling designs on their waistcoats to catch a lady's eye (the cut-steel types were reported to have a hypnotic effect).

You might assume that older buttons are always more valuable, but this is not necessarily so. During the 19th century, many black glass designs were made in imitation of jet, a polished, velvet-black mineral. But despite their age, black glass buttons are hardly collector's items today.

On the other hand, a West German Moonglow style with a gleaming iridescent finish, from the 1950s or 1960s, is highly prized. So spill out that mayonnaise jar and see what treasures you have. Remember that even if a button isn't "worth" anything, sentimental value can make it priceless.

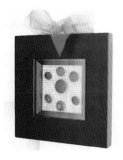

"Realistics" are buttons in the shape of the object they portray. Many, like French celluloid bears, were made in the 1930s (opposite). The string of squares-in-circles is also Art Deco vintage.

Julie Walker, stylist for *Mary Engelbreit's Home Companion*, displays her favorite buttons sewn onto newspaper and mounted in a black-frame shadowbox (above).

When you pin on a metal button, you tell the world a little something about yourself. Perhaps you've served with the Red Cross, had perfect attendance all through high school, or were a member of the Batman & Robin Society in the 1960s. Some collectors show off their stash by grouping them according to color in compartments, supplemented by old soda bottle caps.

A St. Louis social studies teacher's collection of political buttons is not only useful in the classroom but looks striking strewn across a tabletop (left). The older celluloid buttons with paper pictures were made as late as the 1960s and are prized over mass-produced metal. Search for political and campaign buttons in non-election years, when they're cheaper; buttons promoting unusual causes and regional campaigns win the most collector votes.

With the exception of the 1930s porcelain clown face, all the buttons edging a shelf are ordinary sewing box selections, made special as trim for a bathroom vanity (right).

paper
pushers

Original artwork, printed
one color at a time,
once decorated seed
packets (above).

Mary Engelbreit found
these valuable Johnny
Gruelle illustrations
(opposite) at a sale in an
Illinois town. Now she
safeguards them under
glass. When you handle
vintage paper, wear
white cotton gloves.

WHO WANTS YESTERDAY'S PAPERS? PLENTY
of people. Paper mania has rustled through the collecting
world at a fast clip. In fact, there are shows devoted solely to
paper collectibles. As you walk the aisles you'll find sheet
music (very frameable), wine labels, matchbooks, steamboat
time tables, old banknotes in orange and silver emblazoned
with buffaloes and Indian chiefs, expired drivers' licenses and
passports, honeycomb Thanksgiving turkeys, Japanese paper
dolls, playing cards (with Charlie Chaplin as the Joker), even
honorable discharge certificates.

Movie memorabilia is huge. Collectors can snap up quaint
old window cards, which were posted in drugstore and
barbershop windows around town, advertising what was
playing at the local movie house. Movie theatre posters
promoting the films with action-packed scenes and bold
graphics are even more highly coveted.

Of course, a poster doesn't have to feature Gary Cooper
to be popular: there's a whole world of designs advertising
everything from buttons to cheese and car transmissions.
Lithographed, four-color posters proliferated from the 1890s
to World War II, when the technique was replaced by offset

printing. Not surprisingly, these early, more painstakingly created designs are the most-wanted posters of today.

Newspapers, especially those with famous headlines, and magazines are yet another important link in the paper chain. Collectors love them for different reasons—feelings of nostalgia or fascination with an earlier, unknown world.

"Never throw out magazines, though people will tell you the opposite," says *Mary Engelbreit's Home Companion* executive editor Barbara Martin—who protects her cache of 1960s *Esquire* magazines in fireproof flat files. As a photographer, Barbara also prizes vintage photographs, an area likely to boom in future years as collectors scavenge out late 19th- and early 20th-century daguerreotypes, tintypes, and albumin prints.

Other less-than-obvious paper collectibles are handwritten letters, already a dying breed. Remember the old rule of rarity? If it's going to be obsolete, it will be worth more.

Postcards are a collecting destination unto themselves. During their heyday from 1898 to 1918, postcards were created for every holiday, including July 4th and St. Patrick's Day. Some were minor masterpieces, with such details as handtinting, embroidery, and windows that glowed when held to the light. Through postcards, you can feast your eyes on a dining car of the Baltimore & Ohio railroad in 1910 or imagine a holiday at a swanky 1950s resort like The Hotel Breakers in Corpus Christi, "the Naples of the Gulf."

So think twice before you throw out that piece of paper. It could be the start of an obsession.

A cache of 1910 Easter postcards (opposite) are remarkably pristine— probably because they were stored and displayed in special albums, as was the fashion of the day.

In a Gulf Coast home (above), maps of Florida from different eras make it possible to chart state growth over the last hundred years. Some are handcolored and linenbacked, with ornately scrolled text.

Gum wrappers, drawings, Chinese-English flashcards, postcards, pullouts from *Mad* magazine—anything paper!—animate illustrator Lane Smith's studio (left). If you don't want to put pinholes into your treasures, use teacher's putty, a gum-like substance that doesn't leave a residue.

Labels of even the most common household staples, like these from old cans (right), were once decorated with an artist's touch.

united states of
pottery

Unite disparate pieces by focusing on a single shade. The vase at far left (above) is typical of Haeger, founded in 1871 as a brickyard. An art pottery from 1914, Haeger is still in business today. Doublehandled urns and vases were hugely popular. These date from the 1940s (opposite).

IN POTTERY'S PROGRESS, 1890 WAS A VERY good year. Not only was the Roseville Pottery Company founded in Roseville, Ohio, but Rookwood also opened its doors across the state in Cincinnati. Equally impressive, 1899 saw McCoy set up shop in Roseville, and Taylor Smith & Taylor settle in West Virginia. And let's not forget 1909, the year that gave us Bauer in California and Fulper Pottery of Flemington, New Jersey, creators of the state's first art pottery, the Vasekraft line.

Why the sudden flurry of activity all across the country? It was a response to Arts and Crafts fever, which emphasized a return to craftsmanship and spawned an aesthetic revolution.

Of course, we all know that the pottery from that era commands top dollar today. But long after the Arts and Crafts movement seemed passé in the 1920s, most of these potteries chugged on and new ones started, resulting in less arty, more utilitarian wares from the 1930s through the 1960s that are within the reach of the casual collector. In fact, they still turn up in off-the-beaten-path antiques shops today, as generations clear out their cupboards clinking with old wedding gifts.

You're unlikely to find early McCoy artware—for instance, a pedestaled jardiniere with hand-painted flowers—but pitchers, florist's pieces, cookie jars, and vases abound from the 1930s on. So, too, Roseville's early brown-glazed Rozane art pottery vases are slim pickings for the budget-minded, but its sculpture-like White Rose line of bud vases and candlesticks from 1940 ("ideal for bridge parties") is plentiful and affordable.

Don't be surprised if you turn up biomorphic trays, bowls, bases, and candlesticks designed by Russel Wright, best known for his American Modern dinnerware series, its shapes so untraditional that no company sold it for years until Steubenville of Ohio nervously took the plunge. In mix-and-match colors like *seafoam, chartreuse, granite, bean,* and *coral,* the sets outsold all their competitors from 1939 to 1959. Taylor Smith & Taylor immediately issued a challenge with their line of LuRay Pastels in *windsor blue, surf green,* and *sharon pink.*

Also try your luck with Frankoma, founded by John Frank of Oklahoma in 1933. Even if you don't think you're familiar with it, you are: The simple lines of its figurines, vases, and flower pots in mellow browns, golds, and greens are an American icon.

If you're into novelty, seek out Niloak (*kaolin* spelled backwards), made in the Ozarks from 1910 to 1946 and sold in Southwestern tourist stops. With marbleized swirls of desert sunset colors, the vases, ashtrays, and wall pockets were like bringing a piece of America home.

Nesting bowls in ribbed and chevron designs were especially popular in the 1920s through the 1940s (above).

Figural swan vases abounded in the 1940s (opposite). 1950s swans tended to look fluffier, with unruly feathers moving in different directions.

To capture the Deco mood of the 1930s, Bauer introduced batter bowls, eggcups, sherbets, and plates by Ringware— instantly recognizable by its concentric circles. Featuring both pastel matte glazes and dark high-fired glazes, Bauer paved the path for Homer Laughlin's Fiesta. On the windowsill beyond sits mid-20th-century flower and African violet pots as well as butterfly jardinieres from McCoy. Some have been embossed with daisies and dragonflies. If you find what looks like a mix between a jardiniere and a bowl, with two holes in the top rim, it's actually a hanging planter.

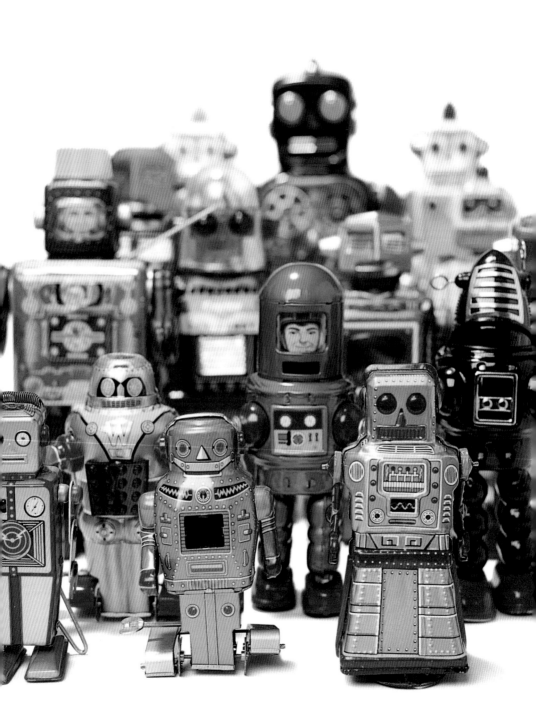

stellar
robots

IF YOU'VE EVER HAD THE URGE TO CHUCK
your *Lost In Space* robot under the chin (if you can find it),
then you probably understand why collectors obsess over
these mechanical men.

The very first robots, from the 1940s and stamped
Occupied Japan, were downright cute. Lore has it that they
were recycled from tins discarded by American soldiers.
The results were riveted, windup affairs that walked
haltingly on individual feet. By the 1950s, wireless remote control was the buzz, with Radicon Robot leading
the way. He glided along on wheels; the slight flare of
his body classifies him as a "skirted" design.

Isaac Asimov's *I, Robot* (1952) portrayed them as
allies and servants of the human race and *Forbidden
Planet's* Robby the Robot (1956) fit that bill. The 1950s
also saw the first plastic designs, produced largely by
Americans. By the 1960s, robots designed to blow smoke
and self-destruct also took on a muscular appearance
(carried on into the 1970s and 1980s). Brawny, faceless
creations, they are nevertheless collectible. Always,
always keep the box.

Non-aggressive, mask-
like faces and "time
machine" bodies with
dials indicate that the
first-row robots (opposite)
are old in robot years,
probably from the 1940s.
Behind them stands a
circa 1958 trash-can style
spaceman of lithographed
metal dressed for a
moonwalk.

This tin man's plain
silver finish indicates a
postwar vintage (above).

garden
variety

AT FIRST GLANCE, IT'S JUST JUNK. RUSTED. Caked with dirt. Missing parts. But old garden stuff is really a Cinderella story, just waiting for the right collector to come along.

Watering cans cultivate a huge audience. The best still have their rose, the term for the detachable sprinkling device. Brass and silverplated brass cans are especially valuable and unusual, though galvanized ones are always appealing. Those mysterious numbers embossed on the bottom—8, 10, 12—refer to how many quarts the can will hold.

Metal, glass, or ceramic flower frogs are another growing area. If they have a maker's mark, so much the better. Collectors tend to use them not for floral displays, but for showing off in a vignette with old rescued gates and trellises and a few garden tools.

Don't forget the furniture—the tubular steel lawn chairs with seashell scalloped backs from the 1940s, wooden work benches and Adirondack chairs, wrought iron and wicker garden settees. You can still pick up a floral-patterned glider here and there: those 1950s types with jaunty fringed sunroofs will never be equalled.

Ornaments from the garden look at home displayed indoors, especially in this sunny potting room (above).

In her sunroom, Mary Engelbreit displays well-weathered birdhouses, some built by farmers and others by roadside artists (opposite).

Tin lithographed children's watering cans date from Victorian times to as recently as the 1970s. Collectors look for images of children in clothes that define an era, whether an Edwardian garden party dress or a 1950s romper. Check underneath as big makers, including toy manufacturers Wolverine and Chein, usually stamped their names on the bottom of the pails. Condition is important, but, naturally—since they're garden tools— rust does take its course. These are especially pristine examples.

globe trotter's
souvenirs

WHERE WOULD YOU LIKE TO GO TODAY?
With souvenirs by your side, you can take a little holiday whenever you like—whether by entering a rodeo scene on a Texas scarf or holding a tiny Washington Monument in your hands.

People have been embarking on these mini-trips since at least the 19th century. Train and boat travel created captive audiences for take-home mementos, from sterling spoons and china cups to plates and easy-to-stow hankies.

When the automobile appeared in the 1920s and 1930s, roadside attractions began to sprout. By the 1940s and 1950s, Americans were traveling the interstates in record numbers. Mom-and-pop gift shops and Indian trading posts flourished, offering cold soda, displays of reptiles or petrified wood, and lots of essentials: beaded belts, linen calendars, salt and pepper shakers, and snowdomes. Later decades still had souvenir shops, of course, but with the appearance of superhighways, it was never the same.

A word to the wise: Souvenirs are priced highest in the environs they tout. So look for mementoes of favorite places anywhere but there. What a great excuse for a road trip!

Made from pot metal (also used for car hood ornaments), a miniature Empire State Building and Statue of Liberty recreate a trip to New York on a desktop (opposite).

The 20th-century globes produced by map companies (above) often have a copyright date and a designer's name printed directly on them, usually off the coast of Australia.

For a sense of international intrigue, stack up suitcases bearing vintage travel stickers (left).

If you crossed a lava lamp with a snow-dome, you'd probably get a floaty pen—in which moving scenes are suspended in a gelatinous liquid (right). An inexpensive modern-day collectible, they could appreciate considerably in value over the coming decades.

Among the first souvenir tumblers were those produced at the World's Columbian Exposition in 1893. They were ruby-stained and engraved with the name and date of the fair. These clear and frosted glass tumblers from the 1960s are decorated with fired-on decals (left).

Mid- to late-20th-century plates from Florida and California show multiple scenes (above). Earlier china celebrated a single image, whether Seminole Indians or sponge divers.

71

treasures
of the sea

Hand-painted wood-
bodied lures are folk art
in their own right (above).
Research their age in old
fishing magazines.

In a Carmel collector's
house, fishing boats dock
in a scene by California
artist Ross Dickinson,
with a mood-setting tray
of sea urchins in the
foreground (opposite).

AT YOUR NEXT AUCTION, DON'T BE SURPRISED
if a sportily clad contingent of local fishing aficionados—
some in wading boots—rubs elbows with the usual band
of antiquers. They're all hooked on a common passion: pre-
1940s hand-tied feather flies, bamboo rods, fitted aluminum
fly tackle boxes, and glass-eyed lures, to name a few.

While a silver reel might start a bidding war, there's a
much less obvious subcurrent you can ply: ordinary items
like minnow buckets, glass floaters (they bob on the water),
and nets are humble treasures awaiting transformation.
Group them in evocative tableaux, perhaps with chalkware
sailor boys and girls from the 1930s, fishing gear pam-
phlets, or steamship schedules. Everyone seems to
have a shoebox of shells and beach glass in the closet.
Display them in a pretty bowl instead. Or show off larger
shells like channeled whelks behind glass in a cabinet,
along with scientific journals and a microscope. Explore
the world of shell folk art. Whether they are Victorian
sewing boxes encrusted with coquinas or cowries from
1930s-era Miami Beach carved with verse, these funky
creations bring out the inner beachcomber in everyone.

Tin lithographed sand pails were manufactured from the late Victorian era until the 1960s, when plastic triumphed. Chein, Ohio Art, and Marx were big makers. Souvenir lettering on two of the pails (above) indicate early 20th century origins. The one in the foreground is vibrantly 1960s. Other pails span the fabulous 1950s (left). With the middle one, the children's dress gives their age away. Rust and denting lower their value.

Toss shells in a big brass tray with a sand-pail shovel for scooping (above left).

Old aquariums are a common sight at garage sales, where ten bucks takes the tank, complete with motor and bagged sand (below left). You needn't add fish; tugboats, sailboats, and sailors are evocative reminders of the sea.

Arranged on a mantelpiece with bright flowers, model ships of varying sizes and subdued natural colors complement each other— and themselves when staggered in front of a large mirror (right).

credits

So many wonderful, creative people have brought us into their homes and shared their collections to inspire us. I would like to thank them from the bottom of my heart.

Mary

PHOTOGRAPHY ON PAGE 8 BY JENIFER JORDAN; PAGES 16-17, 53, AND 60-61 BY ERIC JOHNSON; PAGE 63 BY MIKE JENSEN; PAGE 67 BY JIM HEDRICH; PAGE 72 BY CATHERINE BOGERT; ALL OTHER PHOTOGRAPHY BY BARBARA ELLIOTT MARTIN.

2 COLLECTORS: Nancy and Bill Keenan, Chicago, Illinois

5 COLLECTORS: TOP—Bianca Juarez, Los Angeles, California MIDDLE—Lacy and Bob Buck, Carmel, California BOTTOM—Mary Engelbreit, St. Louis, Missouri; Charlotte Lyons, Irvington, New York; and Jane Crews, Seaside, Florida

6 COLLECTOR: Nelle Smarr, Mexico, Missouri

8 COLLECTORS: Cheryl and Bob Alexander, Alpharetta, Georgia

9 COLLECTORS: Enid Hubbard, Carmel, California; Mary Engelbreit, St. Louis, Missouri; Susan Smith, St. Louis, Missouri; Pat Fischer, St. Louis, Missouri

10 COLLECTORS: Julie and David Walker, St. Louis, Missouri

11 COLLECTOR: Mary Engelbreit, St. Louis, Missouri

12 COLLECTORS: Linda and Stu Davidson, Berkeley Lake, Georgia

13 PICNIC BASKETS from Stone Ledge Antiques, Dutzow, Missouri, (314) 458-3516

14 COLLECTOR: Mary Engelbreit, St. Louis, Missouri

15 COLLECTOR: Vincent Flewellen, St. Louis, Missouri

16-17 COLLECTOR: Connie Copley, St. Louis, Missouri

18 COLLECTOR: Patricia Brangle, St. Louis, Missouri

19 COLLECTORS: Janet and Tom Proch, Fredericksburg, Texas

20 COLLECTOR: Jackie Spicer, Los Angeles, California

21 COLLECTOR: Dominique Pfahl, San Francisco, California

22 COLLECTORS: TOP LEFT—Patricia Brangle, St. Louis, Missouri BOTTOM LEFT—Rod and Jill Perth, San Marino, California

23 COLLECTORS: Belinda and Jesika Hare, Fredericksburg, Texas

24 COLLECTORS: Julie and Henry Kelston, Nyack, New York

26 COLLECTOR: Pamela M. Mullin, Santa Barbara, California

27 COLLECTOR: Mary Engelbreit, St. Louis, Missouri

28-29 BOOKS from Kitchen Arts & Letters, Inc., New York, New York, (212) 876-5550; Rick Moore Antiques, St. Louis, Missouri, (314) 390-2618; Food Heritage Press, Ipswich, Massachusetts, (508) 356-8306; Charlotte F. Safir, New York, New York, (212) 534-7933; Barbara A. Weindling, P. O. Box 368, Bridgewater, Connecticut, 06752

30 COLLECTORS: Lacy and Bob Buck, Carmel, California

32 COLLECTOR: Paul Cavalli, St. Louis, Missouri

33   COLLECTOR: Joseph Slattery, St. Louis, Missouri

34   COLLECTORS: Lacy and Bob Buck, Carmel, California

35   COLLECTORS: Marie and Bill Trader, Chicago, Illinois

36   COLLECTORS: Rod and Jill Perth, San Marino, California

37   COLLECTOR: Christina Donna, Larkspur, California

38   COLLECTORS: Alice Newquist, Fort Lauderdale, Florida; Mary Engelbreit, St. Louis, Missouri

39   COLLECTOR: Bianca Juarez, Los Angeles, California

40   COLLECTORS: Marie and Bill Trader, Chicago, Illinois

41   COLLECTORS: TOP—Alice Newquist, Fort Lauderdale, Florida; Mary Engelbreit, St. Louis, Missouri

ARTISAN: BOTTOM—Stacey Stucky, Rancho Santa Margarita, California

42   COLLECTOR: Jackie Spicer, Los Angeles, California

43   COLLECTORS: Julie and David Walker, St. Louis, Missouri

44   COLLECTORS: Roberta and David Williamson, Berea, Ohio

46   COLLECTOR: Vincent Flewellen, St. Louis, Missouri

47   COLLECTOR: Mary Engelbreit, St. Louis, Missouri

48   COLLECTOR: Suzy Mueller, London, England

49-50   COLLECTOR: Mary Engelbreit, St. Louis, Missouri

51   COLLECTOR: Becky Portera, Seaside, Florida

52   COLLECTOR: Lane Smith, New York, New York

53   TULIP BULB TRAY from 22nd/Second Warehouse, Houston, Texas, (713) 864-0261 BUTTERFLY PINS, toys, bugs, kaleidoscope from méli mélo, (314) 725-4285, St. Louis, Missouri ROUND BUTTERFLY PINS from Maximal Art, Philadelphia, Pennsylvania, (800) 573-3308 LABELS AND BOTANICAL PRINTS from Warson Woods Antiques Gallery, St. Louis, Missouri,

(314) 909-0123 NEW ZEALAND envelope and butterfly postcard series from www.ebay.com

54   COLLECTORS: Carol and Terry Crouppen, St. Louis, Missouri

55   COLLECTOR: Mary Engelbreit, St. Louis, Missouri

56   COLLECTOR: Marcy Spanogle, St. Louis, Missouri

57   COLLECTORS: Nancy and Bill Keenan, Chicago, Illinois

58   COLLECTOR: Sandy Koepke, Topanga Canyon, California

60   COLLECTOR: Bill Hibdon, St. Louis, Missouri

61   COLLECTOR: Mary Engelbreit, St. Louis, Missouri

62   COLLECTOR: Candy Moger, Seattle, Washington

63   COLLECTOR: Mary Engelbreit, St. Louis, Missouri

64   COLLECTOR: Enid Hubbard, Carmel, California

66   COLLECTOR: Terri Farrell, St. Louis, Missouri

67   COLLECTOR: Esther Fishman, Chicago, Illinois

68   COLLECTOR: Marcy Spanogle, St. Louis, Missouri

69   COLLECTORS: Julie and Henry Kelston, Nyack, New York

70-71   COLLECTOR: Terri Farrell, St. Louis, Missouri; SOUVENIRS from Stone Ledge Antiques, Dutzow, Missouri, (314) 458-3516

72   COLLECTOR: Toby and Stephen Schachman, Long Beach Island, New Jersey

73   COLLECTORS: Lacy and Bob Buck, Carmel, California

74-75   COLLECTORS: Mary Engelbreit, St. Louis, Missouri; Charlotte Lyons, Irvington, New York; Jane Crews, Seaside, Florida

76   COLLECTORS: TOP—Becky Portera, Seaside, Florida BOTTOM—Mary Engelbreit, St. Louis, Missouri

77   COLLECTOR: Pamela M. Mullin, Santa Barbara, California

80   COLLECTOR: Bianca Juarez, Los Angeles, California